THE METAPHYSICALS
AND MILTON

THE METAPHYSICALS
AND MILTON

BY

E. M. W. TILLYARD

LITT.D., F.B.A.
Master of Jesus College
Cambridge

GREENWOOD PRESS, PUBLISHERS
WESTPORT, CONNECTICUT

Library of Congress Cataloging in Publication Data

Tillyard, Eustace Mandeville Wetenhall, 1889-1962.
  The metaphysicals and Milton.

    Reprint of the ed. published by Chatto & Windus,
London.
    1. English poetry--Early modern, 1500-1700--History
and criticism--Addresses, essays, lectures. 2. Milton,
John, 1608-1674--Criticism and interpretation--Addresses,
essays, lectures. 3. Donne, John, 1572-1631--Criticism
and interpretation--Addresses, essays, lectures. I. Ti-
tle.
[PR544.T5   1975   821'.009   75-31444
ISBN 0-8371-8515-7

Originally published in 1956 by Chatto & Windus, London

Reprinted with the permission of Chatto & Windus, Ltd.

Reprinted in 1975 by Greenwood Press,
a division of Williamhouse-Regency Inc.

Library of Congress Catalog Card Number 75-31444

ISBN 0-8371-8515-7

Printed in the United States of America

PREFACE

I WROTE the following text in response to an invitation from the University of Washington to be Walker-Ames Lecturer there in the academic year 1955–6; and I wish to thank the University authorities for their kindness in supplying this incentive and Professor Heilman and his colleagues for making my consequent visit to Seattle a singularly happy one.

Keeping lecture requirements in view, I have studied to suggest rather than to argue closely, and to arrive at general observations however much I have used particular poems as aids on my way.

E. M. W. T.

Jesus College
Cambridge

v

CONTENTS

INTRODUCTION

SINCE Donne was rediscovered some thirty-five years ago, critics and scholars have written a great deal about the Metaphysical poets. Nor, because he has not needed rediscovery, have they spared Milton the same treatment. On the other hand, they have written a good deal less about the *relations* of the Metaphysicals and Milton; and the opinions men have held on those relations have been liable to change and are still in a state of flux. There is more room for lectures on both topics together than for lectures on either in isolation.

In the early days of revived enthusiasm for the Metaphysicals, Milton, so firmly established, the vast oak not giving the smaller shrubs near by their place in the sun, was conceived of as a kind of enemy; and Donne was the man to put up against him. As in any new stir of thought, the partisan spirit showed itself; and some admirers of Donne joined to dilate his claims to greatness and to undermine the top-heavy reputation of the established idol. George Williamson's book on the Donne tradition (1930), written when the enthusiasm for the Metaphysicals was at its height, is typical of this spirit. If Milton was ever good at anything, he gave you to understand, Donne was always a bit better. This partisan enthusiasm has waned since then but it has left its effects. People still unconsciously conceive of an opposition between the Metaphysical school and Milton, in spite of a growing realisation that it is perilous to talk of schools of poets at all in the first half of the seventeenth century.

The main object of these lectures is to examine this supposed opposition. Some sort of opposition there undoubtedly is; but I fancy we are apt to be wrong in what we oppose to what. My belief is that the opposition of Metaphysicals to Milton is less than the opposition of the extraordinary temperament of Donne to the temperaments of the other poets of his time or shortly after, whether these poets did or did not fall under the influence of Donne's rhetoric. Milton too had a most decided character, but since, as a poet, he submitted it more truly to the demands of his age, he is in most ways closer to it than Donne was to his. In fact, in this matter he resembled another man of a most decided character, Ben Jonson. Donne, it is true, imposed his lyrical rhetoric on many poets but he never imposed on them the peculiar pattern of his mind. Even so immediate, and apparently so indebted, a follower of Donne as Herbert is in many motions of his mind nearer to Milton.

A good way to enter my ground is to compare the sonnets which Donne and Milton wrote to their deceased wives. In 1601, at the age of twenty-nine, Donne had begun to make his fortune in the world of affairs. He was Member of Parliament and secretary to a leading politician, Sir Thomas Egerton, keeper of the great seal. Egerton was a widower; and living in the house was his wife's niece and adopted daughter,

Anne More, aged sixteen. Donne and the girl fell in
love and were secretly married in December 1601.
Through this rash act Donne alienated his patron and
ruined his career as a man of affairs. Ultimately he
attained a stable position in life as Dean of St. Paul's.
But that was not till 1621. His wife lived to see him
become priest, but four years before he became Dean
she died, having borne him twelve children in the
sixteen years of their married life. By worldly standards
she had fared badly, her marriage having missed both
periods of Donne's prosperity. But the match was a
love match, and from his letters it seems that he had a
tender conscience concerning her welfare. Here is the
sonnet celebrating her death.

> Since she whom I lov'd hath paid her last debt
> To nature and to hers, and my good is dead,
> And her soul early into heaven ravished,
> Wholly in heavenly things my mind is set.
> Here the admiring her my mind did whet
> To seek Thee, God; so streams do show the head:
> But though I have found Thee, and Thou my
>   thirst hast fed,
> A holy thirsty dropsy melts me yet.
> But why should I beg more love, whenas Thou
> Dost woo my soul, for hers off'ring all Thine,
> And dost not only fear lest I allow
> My love to saints and angels, things divine,
> But in Thy tender jealousy dost doubt
> Lest the world, flesh, yea devil put Thee out? [1]

[1] For discussion of some difficult places in this sonnet see Appendix
A, 75.

As in most of Donne the argument cannot be grasped entire at a first hearing; so I will outline the sequence of thought. 'My wife, whom I loved, is dead, snatched away, still young, to heaven; with the result that my own mind is quite set on heavenly things. While she lived, my admiration for her led me to God, as a stream can be traced to its source. But though I have thus found God, and he has satisfied my thirst for him, I still crave thirstily the love of my wife.' Here, let it be noted, Donne goes back on his statement that his mind is quite set on heavenly things. And he proceeds: 'But, after all, it is irrelevant expecting more love from my dead wife, when God is offering me *all* his love instead of her *broken* affection. And this love is comprehensive, for it claims to dispossess not only my holy love of my dead wife but my wicked love of the world, the flesh, and the Devil.'

Like all Donne's poems, this sonnet prompts many thoughts. I will confine my comments to three.

First, it is a self-centred sonnet. It is about his own feelings and the state of his own soul and his hopes of what God is going to do for it. His dead wife, the nominal concern of the sonnet, is not in the least characterised, she really has no existence (in spite of the elopement and the twelve children in sixteen years), and she is the mere passive vehicle of her husband's self-preoccupations. Along with the self-centred thought goes the entirely characteristic run of the verse: the drawn-out rhythms, the halting intensity. Like so much else of Donne, this sonnet is exclusively *his*, unmitigatedly individual; it gives the sense, one could almost say the smell, of his unescapable personality, a personality that can grip, charm, stun, even overwhelm. C. S. Lewis has written of Donne's 'exacting quality', his 'urgency and pressure upon the reader in every line'.[1] Contrariwise, Donne shows no social sense. He does not set his wife in any large human context.

Secondly, there is the logical structure. Donne begins by making a very decided statement:

Wholly in heavenly things my mind is set.

He then goes back on this decided statement by adding that

A holy thirsty dropsy melts me yet,

the thirst being for a human, though holy, love. And he ends by showing that neither the decided statement nor the contradiction of it is to the point, because his wife's love for him has been superseded by the infinitely inclusive love of God. This kind of logical structure is quite characteristic of Donne and implies an unusual cast of mind; a reluctance to reach conclusions, a keener relish for the processes than for the issues of thought, a cast of mind the remotest possible from the sphere of action.

The third matter is the rhetoric, and especially the close relation of the sense and the speaking voice. The sonnet is not one of Donne's greatest and it does not get into Grierson's *Metaphysical Poetry Donne to Butler*. 'Holy thirsty dropsy' from the line just quoted strikes

[1] *Seventeenth Century Studies presented to Sir Herbert Grierson* (Oxford, 1938) 69.

me as rather silly in sound, though its defenders might say it mimicked the monotony of dripping water. Nevertheless Donne's great gift of appearing to think aloud shows itself here. One of his most common and his most characteristic means to this end is his ability to slow down his rhythms, which gives the air of his being in the very gestation of thought or of being impeded in it by the very strength of his emotions. The first three lines succeed wonderfully, in their slow and halting gait, in rendering the stupefaction of intense grief, of the dreadful effort required to make it articulate:

> Sinće shé/whom I lóv'd/hath paíd/her lást/débt [1]
> To nát/ure añd/to hérs,/and my goód/is déad,
> And her sóul/eaŕly/into heá/ven ráv/ishéd—.

Only in the fourth line,

> Wholly in heavenly things my mind is set,

does he emerge into unstupefied thought and a clear rhythm. It is as if with the dreadful word *ravished*, coming like a choked sob after a pause, he has controlled his grief and can use a normal intonation. I am not saying that Donne personally felt like this when he wrote this sonnet. There is a rhetoric of the familiar style quite as much as of the hieratic; and by 1617 he was an old hand at his pet effects. Whatever Donne was doing here he was not being spontaneous and 'natural'. On the contrary he studies his effects to the full. The point is that he brings them off. Donne also

[1] I read this line differently from Helen Gardner, *Donne, the Divine Poems* (Oxford, 1952) 78.

sets one division of his sonnet pointedly and beautifully against the other. In the octave the verse is clotted, but with 'But why should I . . .' it becomes thin, clear, exalted, betokening a cleansed state of the spirit.

So much, at present, for Donne's sonnet.

In 1656 Milton, now aged forty-eight and four years a widower, married Katharine Woodcock, a woman of twenty-eight belonging to a good but impoverished family. Fifteen months later she and her infant daughter died; and, to quote Samuel Johnson, 'her husband has honoured her in a poor sonnet'. Here is this sonnet that Johnson thought ill of:

Methought I saw my late espoused saint
Brought to me like Alcestis from the grave,
Whom Jove's great son to her glad husband gave,
Rescued from Death by force, though pale and faint.
Mine, as whom, wash'd from spot of child-bed taint,
Purification in the old law did save,
And such as yet once more I trust to have
Full sight of her in heaven without restraint,
Came vested all in white, pure as her mind.
Her face was veiled; yet to my fancied sight
Love, sweetness, goodness in her person shined
So clear, as in no face with more delight.
But oh, as to embrace me she inclined,
I wak'd, she fled, and day brought back my night.

It is possible to find fault with this sonnet. The fifth line halts for no apparent reason; and it and the next line have too little the air of coming of themselves. But the poem gathers strength; its elements unite to

7

build up a climax; and it ends poignantly. Whatever its faults, it is not a poor sonnet. And, what most matters now, it is true to the poetical character of its author. If I compare it with Donne's sonnet on a similar subject I shall be making a wider comparison: one between two different poetic methods and two different poetic personalities.

Asking now how Milton's sonnet compares with Donne's I say first that Milton has his eye on his deceased wife and not on himself. True, he refers in the last line to his blindness. But the line is intelligible without the personal reference, for *night* also means the spiritual gloom created in Milton's mind by his wife's death. Indeed, the sonnet is at odds with the common idea of Milton as a proud, egotistical man. It centres on the subject it proposes and treats her as a real woman, doing her high honour. Even so, Milton carefully keeps the public decencies. In dreaming that the loved one was not dead after all, Milton probably records a personal experience. But it is a common thing for bereaved people to dream so, while the theme had already occurred among the Italian sonneteers, thus becoming public property. Further, Milton removes any possible scandal of over-privacy by the august context in which he places his wife; for he compares her first to a Greek queen and then to one of the ancient archetypes of religious practice in the old Hebrew world. In actual life Katharine Woodcock seems to have been an ordinary, if amiable, middle-class woman; yet such was the support Milton enjoyed from contemporary

convention that he could work this surprising approximation without the least suspicion of being ridiculous.
The still massive humanism of the seventeenth century
not merely allowed but encouraged him to arrogate
such dignity to an ordinary mortal of his own time.
Indeed, in doing this he was respecting an obligation
to society, the obligation to assert the dignity of man.
Johnson hated Milton's politics and thought some of
his poetical mannerisms too individual, but he accepted
him as sound on the poet's obligation to society, the
matter in which he thought the Metaphysicals most
offended.

Secondly, in his logical structure, though Milton
varies his thought he never turns back on himself, as
Donne does. He begins with a comparison that serves
as far as it goes. His wife was indeed like Alcestis whom
Heracles brought back, pale and faint, from the dead.
But 'pale and faint' leads to a second thought. His wife's
pallor and faintness befit the ceremony of Purification
as ordained by the Mosaic books, a ceremony that took
place not long after the birth of the child, when the
mother had not recovered all her strength, and which
demanded the wearing of a white robe. The Hebrew
reference thus does not contradict but reinforces that to
Greek tragedy; as it should do, being more holy and
belonging to a realm higher than the more natural
realm of classical antiquity. But Milton gives the vision
a higher connotation still. His wife's appearance was
that of her resurrected and glorified body. From such
height the poet can only descend; and he adds that the

virtues which shone in her person, love sweetness goodness, prolonged of course in heaven, were yet her
attributes on earth. And the descent from Paradise to
earth fitly suggests the parallel descent from ecstatic
dream to the cruel actuality of present bereavement.
Milton does not rush to his end; he embellishes the
way to it; but he has it steadily in mind.

In the interesting *Notes on Donne* [1] Allen Tate advances
but does not answer the question whether 'the local
excitement of sensation will indefinitely obscure the
formal qualities of the Spenserian-Miltonic verse'. I
say nothing at present about any answer to this question
and merely record that 'local excitement of sensation'
describes the effect of Donne's rhetoric very well, while
the 'formal qualities of the Spenserian-Miltonic verse'
are readily apparent in Milton's sonnet to his dead wife.
Not that Milton's rhetoric is at all monotonous or
consistently smooth and dulcet. There is, for instance,
a clear and beautiful contrast between the exalted
smoothness of the first line,

> Methought I saw my late espoused saint,

apt to the joyful vision, and the abrupt rhythm of the
last line,

> I wak'd, she fled, and day brought back my night,

describing the shattering of his happy fancy. But the
contrast is not so staged as to give the sense of something
thought out on the spot, in the very act of utterance.
It rests on a rhetoric of emotion, solidly grounded in

[1] In *Reactionary Essays on Poetry and Ideas* (New York, 1936) 68.

reason and human nature, publicly ratified, and, in the best sense of the word, conventional. Again, the middle of the sonnet, describing the wife in terms of the Old Testament and of Paradise, and syntactically the most complicated and sustained rhetorical unit, makes no effort to simulate a speaker finding his way through a difficult argument in improvised discourse and is, quite frankly, a construction, and a construction the legitimacy of which was not in 1658 in the least called in doubt. Thus, while Milton's rhetoric forgoes 'the local excitement of sensation' it acknowledges its obligation to the grand code of rules laid down by the contemporary republic of letters. For Milton, who had an extremely sensitive social conscience, this was liberty; a willing conformity to laws based on the universal principles of human reason.

I now go on to some of the general topics that the comparison of the two sonnets has raised.

2

PERSONAL AND PUBLIC

WHEN I said that Donne in the sonnet under review was apparently more interested in the condition of his own soul than in the character of his wife, any suggestion of surprise that may have been insinuated had nothing to do with this interest in itself. In examining the condition of his soul Donne was fulfilling the age-long Christian injunction of knowing yourself, of turning the eye inward from the outer world to the fallen self. He was carrying out the injunctions of St. Augustine's *Soliloquies* and St. Bernard's *Meditations* and he was doing, after the fashion of his own religious tradition, what some of his contemporary Calvinists were doing in theirs. The surprise consists in Donne's using a sonnet to his dead wife for such a purpose. There is in fact something extreme about Donne: he was apt to exploit a single element at the expense of others; where Milton was less specialised, open to more of the general motions of thought belonging to his age.

I may have sounded unfair in noting a lack of social sense in Donne's sonnet; the sonnet not being a form in which you would expect to find it. But even if I did I was pointing to something generally lacking in him. In his poetry he shows little trace of that sense of public or social obligation which, largely inherited from Greece and Rome in the sixteenth century, was destined to reach its height a century and a half later. The briefest glance at *King Henry IV* and *Hamlet* together will show that it was possible to combine the public and the introspective sides in an eminent degree. And in a less eminent degree, the same combination is found in the *Alchemist* and *Sejanus*. Donne was weak in the values that rule *Sejanus* and *Henry IV*. But, since he is so very strong on the side of mental processes, and since there are other poets than Donne to satisfy where he is weak, we should do ill to complain. And instead of complaining I will go on to talk of a poem that illustrates with peculiar felicity Donne's habit of showing his self-centred interest in the workings of his own mind, the *Blossom*. And I choose to talk of it not only to illustrate Donne's introspection, what Allen Tate calls his habit of pitting his ideas against one another like characters in a play, but also to present the kind of excellence in Donne most likely to survive a long bout of special popularity that cannot in the nature of things suffer no decline. Donne wrote no comprehensive long poem; and no single poem of his can contain all the poetic parts he commands. The *Blossom* is not a religious poem like the sonnet to his dead wife, nor does it approach the fierce absorption of passions into a single monotony that makes the *Nocturnal upon St. Lucy's Day* so notable. But it displays an unusual variety and it reveals the divisions of Donne's personality in the most obvious form. I can imagine that at some future date the *Blossom* will continue to charm while the *Nocturnal* will be treated with a mixture of astonishment and dislike.

The dramatic situation presented in the *Blossom* is the following. Donne is in the country and next day, very early, he will set out for London. There, in London, he knows there is an accommodating lady, ready to return affection, physical and mental. But his perverse heart is not interested and has chosen to pay its attention, in foolish delusion that it may succeed, to a woman in this country neighbourhood whom it has no business to court and who repels his advances. And she is not even particularly desirable. She is cold mentally and physically; and though, Donne conjectures, she might develop on the purely sensual side she will never turn out sincerely affectionate. And Donne's conclusion is: 'What a fool I am! But there it is; that's what I'm like. That's the sort of silly trick the human mind insists on playing.' To express the mind divided within itself Donne adopts the antique method of the disputation; only here it is not two persons or allegorised qualities that dispute but the portions of a single brain. It is the method employed by Marvell in his *Dialogue between the Soul and Body* and by Yeats in his *Dialogue of Self and Soul*. Donne does not dramatise as completely as Yeats; he does not label the speakers and confine his poem to their words. He introduces in his own words the speech that his heart makes. And now for the way the poem evolves.

Donne begins by addressing his heart through two stanzas, the first presenting an analogy with the case his heart is in, an analogy with a blossom, and the second being a direct address to that heart. It is a surprising beginning because it is smoothly lyrical and it is beautiful much in the way the conventional Elizabethan lyric is beautiful. Donne says, as it were: I know by this time you expect me to begin violently and in a way no ordinary writer of lyrics habitually does, something like 'For God's sake, hold your tongue and let me love' or 'He is stark mad whoever says . . .' but this time I am giving another surprise, disappointing what you have come to expect of me; I am being lyrical and incantatory. Further, I enjoy showing you that I am able to do this kind of old-fashioned stuff if I please; possibly better than any of you.

> Little think'st thou, poor flower,
>   Whom I have watch'd six or seven days,
> And seen thy birth and seen what every hour
> Gave to thy growth, thee to this height to raise,
> And now dost laugh and triumph on this bough,
>   Little think'st thou
> That it will freeze anon, and that I shall
> Tomorrow find thee fallen or not at all.
>
> Little think'st thou, poor heart,
>   That labour'st yet to nestle thee
> And think'st by hovering here to get a part
> In a forbidden or forbidding tree,
> And hop'st her stiffness by long siege to bow,
>   Little think'st thou
> That thou tomorrow, ere that sun doth wake,
> Must with this sun and me a journey take.

Notice also how in these stanzas Donne not only sweetens his rhythms but in the second stanza dwells on his images less insistently than usual. The lady is first a tree in which his heart tries birdlike to build a nest, she quickly becomes the conventional image of the fortress besieged by the lover, and finally the regal sun with the hint that the lover's efforts do no damage to the calm and length of her slumbers. Donne deliberately tones down his own metaphorical habits and approximates them to the conventional. But in being thus conventional he is also being satirical towards his heart; he as it were mimics the Petrarchian sentiments of hopeless adoration which his heart has been silly enough to experience.

He goes on to say: of course my heart will have its retort to this—

> But thou, which lov'st to be
> Subtle to plague thyself, wilt say—

and the heart's retort is that it prefers to stay near the lady while the body goes to London; with the implication that love is a purely spiritual business, a superior Platonic affair that can dispense with the physical presences. But note that Donne's heart does not use the lyrical vein that Donne had assumed in addressing it. No, it uses the speech-rhythms normal to Donne's argumentation and it drops all metaphors.

> Alas, if *you* must go, what's that to *me*?
> Here lies my business, and here I will stay:
> You go to friends, whose love and means present
> > Various content
> To your eyes, ears, and tongue, and every part.
> If then your body go, what need you a heart?

Is it over-ingenious to guess that, as Donne's speech to his heart in the opening stanzas mimics ironically the Petrarchian sentiments that heart is foolish enough to feel, the heart counter-attacks by putting *its* case in the unaureate idiom that Donne habitually affects?

Then, in the two final stanzas, Donne has the last word: a contemptuous snort that his heart is quite self-deceived about the ways of women and a piece of advice. *They* have no use for the refinements of disembodied or Platonic love. The woman you're pursuing, says Donne, won't know *my* heart from another's in separation from my body; indeed she won't recognise you for a heart at all, because not having one she has no idea what a heart is like. Any further possibilities in her lie elsewhere. So my advice is: wait a bit here, if you will; then join me in London, where all the rest of me will have had a holiday from female society and will be in fine condition. If you are wise, you will imitate this rest of me to your great advantage. And when we've made it up, there is someone waiting to welcome my reunited self.

> Well then, stay here; but know,
> When thou hast stay'd and done thy most,
> A naked thinking heart, that makes no show,
> Is to a woman but a kind of ghost.
> How shall she know *my* heart, or, having none,
>   Know *thee* for one?
> Practice may make her know some other part,
> But, take my word, she doth not know a heart.

Meet me in London, then,
Twenty days hence, and thou shalt see
Me fresher and more fat by being with men
Than if I had stay'd still with her and thee.
For God's sake, if you can, be you so too:
    I would give you
There to another friend, whom we shall find
As glad to have my body as my mind.

There is a delightful variety in the poem. The first stanzas, however self-consciously planned, convey the element of trance and the refusal to face the facts that the experience of being in love engenders. The total poem also conveys the truth that people very much in love and embarrassed by it can, notwithstanding, exercise their other faculties normally. (It was not Parnell's grand-scale love-affair that ruined him as a politician; indeed it may have stimulated other sides of him to special activity: the ruin came from what other people thought of it, when it became public). The whole tone is cynical, but no complete cynic could have achieved the lyrical beauty of the opening.

There are special reasons too why the *Blossom* should be widely liked. Though the evident work of Donne at his best and of no one else, it is less extreme in manifesting its author's favourite literary habits than most of his great lyrics. Donne could be heavy-handed and inflict his personality on you. But here he manipulates his matter deftly and elegantly; without applying undue pressure. There is even a touch of social consideration. He seems to mitigate his personal obsessions for the reader's

benefit. His cleverness, though not free from exhibition-
ism, does not seek merely to dazzle or stun but is accom-
modated to the ordinary reader. Best of all he apologises
for his divided mind by referring to it explicitly:

> But thou which lov'st to be
> Subtle to plague thyself . . .

It is only a minority of men who are bored with the
normal range of the mind and need the torture of
feeling, the ramifications of self-questioning, or the
exploration of the fringes of consciousness bordering
on the insane to awaken their interest. Most people
think that life offers enough interest through the plagues
it brings along in its ordinary course to make the
subtlety to plague yourself superfluous. In those two
lines Donne pays tribute to this majority feeling,
reprimanding his heart for being so foolish. Finally,
the *Blossom* goes back on itself only once (when Donne
decides that his heart doesn't after all have to leave the
country but can stay there) and genuinely leads up to
a conclusion. There is what can be called a normal
distribution of energy between journey and arrival,
between means and end.

But, though there are reasons why the *Blossom*
should be unusually acceptable to the reader not speci-
ally prejudiced in favour of Donne's personal and
rhetorical peculiarities,[1] its first claim to excellence is

---

[1] The *Ecstasy* is another such poem. I had no space in my lectures to
comment on it; and instead I reprint in Appendix B (77) my note on
the poem published in the *Review of English Studies*, 1943, 67-70.

in the distinction and subtlety of mind it presents to our inspection. Although Donne may make allowance for his readers and in so doing show some social consideration, he is still far from the sense of public, not to say political, obligation that you find in the odes of Horace and even in some of the later Yeats.

To make still clearer these qualities which in spite of various mitigations appear in the *Blossom*, self-questioning and absence of social sense, I turn to a poem more extreme, more typical, and one of his greatest, *A Nocturnal upon St. Lucy's Day*. It is a difficult poem and has called forth much comment. There is, for instance, an exposition of it by W. A. Murray in an article called *Donne and Paracelsus*.[1] It seems that some of the terms Donne uses cannot be understood fully except in the light of Paracelsus's scientific theories. On the other hand the general trend of the poem is plain, and we do not need any Paracelsan knowledge to understand the drift of such a line as

The general balm th' hydroptic earth hath drunk.

General balm has a technical meaning in Paracelsus, which Donne meant to include, but for poetical appreciation we can satisfy ourselves pretty well when we interpret it as a life-giving property generally and take the line to mean that this property has withdrawn into the earth to the utmost extent. Further, no one is likely to quarrel with W. A. Murray's description of the poem's theme as being 'the annihilation of spirit, the

[1] *Review of English Studies*, 1949.

death-in-life which follows supreme loss'. The poem is typically true to Donne's peculiar cast of mind because his feeling increases as the thought becomes more complicated. In the culminating fourth stanza, when Donne describes the supreme nothingness to which the death of his beloved has reduced him (supreme compared with the lesser nothingnesses he had before experienced), the rhythm throbs more and more with emotion as he runs through the different hierarchies of creation, all of them, even the humblest, positive in some way, as he is not, to justify the colossal fantasy of his being the elixir or quintessence of the primal nothingness out of which God created the universe:

> But I am by her death (which word wrongs her)
> Of the first nothing the elixir grown.
>   Were I a man, that I were one
>   I needs must know; I should prefer,
>   If I were any beast,
> Some ends, some means; yea plants, yea stones detest
> And love: all, all some properties invest.
> If I an ordinary nothing were,
> As shadow, a light and body must be there.
>
> But I am none.

Note how Donne goes back on himself in the first line: she is dead, but of course she is not dead, being in heaven. He has leisure to be paradoxical even in the height of passion. But the paradox does not compromise the passion, which we should never dream of doubting to be authentic. On the contrary it has its emotional effect, which is to join with the other extravagances to impress on us the extraordinary cast of Donne's mind. And we watch that mind as if it were some unusual natural portent, a flood, a great wind, an eruption.

I ask you now to consider these two poems of Donne, and especially the *Nocturnal*, along with two poems by other men. The first is Goldsmith's *Traveller*. This is a poem based on living experience, for Goldsmith spent some two years drifting round western Europe on foot, the best possible way of learning the intimacies of a country. But, far from rendering any personal experience, he yields to the excessive social bent of his time and effaces every indication of giving an authentic, first-hand, personal account. Here is how he describes the Swiss, having just dealt with the Italians:

> My soul, turn from them; turn we to survey
> Where rougher climes a nobler race display,
> Where the bleak Swiss their stormy mansion tread,
> And force a churlish soil for scanty bread;
> No product here the barren hills afford,
> But man and steel, the soldier and his sword;
> No vernal blooms their torpid rocks array,
> But winter lingering chills the lap of May;
> No Zephyr fondly sues the mountain's breast,
> But meteors glare, and stormy glooms invest.

This, one would say, shows every sign of having been constructed from one of the old-fashioned school-books in geography: those delightful simple manuals that pictured places in memorable and decisive terms: Holland with canals and windmills and industrious women scrubbing their doorsteps, Paris gay and never going to bed, Switzerland replete with beetling crags and avalanches, Italy a land where the sun always shines and sunburnt peasants spend their time singing *Santa Lucia*, or Canada given over to snow and beavers and general pioneering. You can see how well Goldsmith has succeeded in cutting out all personal reality by comparing accounts in the same poem of places which he had not visited. Goldsmith did not know the Tropics, but his account of them has just the tone of his account of Italy, which he knew uncommonly well.

> The naked negro, panting at the line,
> Boasts of his golden sands and palmy wine,
> Basks in the glare, or stems the tepid wave,
> And thanks his gods for all the good they gave.

If Donne is uncompromisingly personal, Goldsmith goes right to the other extreme and errs in abandoning every advantage in vividness that the exploitation of the personal offered him.

My other comparison leads to more fundamental matters. Donne's *Nocturnal* described sensations of loneliness and annihilation; and now put it alongside another poem in its way equally fantastic and dealing with the same sensations, Coleridge's *Ancient Mariner*. The mariner, becalmed and among the dead, is, humanly, utterly alone:

> Alone, alone, all, all alone,
> Alone on a wide wide sea!
> And never a saint took pity on
> My soul in agony.

23

Further, when he has slept and the curse begins to relax its hold, he is less than a man, a species of nothing:

I moved, and could not feel my limbs:
I was so light—almost
I thought that I had died in sleep,
And was a blesséd ghost.

What then is the final effect on the mind of the two accounts of spiritual annihilation? In answering such naked and uncompromising critical questions it is vain to argue or to cite this or that statement in the texts. All the reader can do is to open himself as best he can to the impact of the poetry, to the impact of the sum of all its parts, and then to record his impression. It may be that my own impression is coloured by the likes and dislikes, the particular receptiveness and the particular aversions of the generation to which I belong. I was brought up on the Romantics and I did not begin to read Donne seriously till I was thirty. But now school-boys read Donne in the higher forms of some British secondary schools; and I can imagine that to a boy who has been taught to accept Donne as a norm the direct and simple contrasts of the *Ancient Mariner* may present themselves as rather ingenuous and not to be seriously enjoyed by a person desperately anxious to pass as an adult. In fact Coleridge would stand to Donne as the simplicities of the fairy-tale stand to the sophistications of the up-to-date story of adventure; and a schoolboy, bred to the Metaphysicals, might feel as much ashamed in confessing to a preference for Coleridge as he would be, if a friend caught him reading the *Red Fairy Book* on the sly. For myself, I think it monstrous that boys should be introduced to the perplexities and the torture of Donne's mind too young. The simpler pessimism of Housman (if you want pessimism) suits the adolescent digestion better, while Coleridge (like the fairy-tale) is both so simple and so profound that he can be enjoyed at every stage of life.

To revert to my impression of these two great accounts of spiritual annihilation: Coleridge expresses the cosmic terror, potential or realised, of all men: Donne expresses the peculiar feeling of annihilation of a very extraordinary man. I do not think it accidental that the *Ancient Mariner* begins and ends in social life, and (at the end) in a social life that includes the animals.

> O Wedding-Guest! this soul hath been
> Alone on a wide wide sea:
> So lonely 'twas, that God himself
> Scarce seeméd there to be.

> O sweeter than the marriage-feast,
> 'Tis sweeter far to me,
> To walk together to the kirk
> With a goodly company!—

> .   .   .   .

> He prayeth best, who loveth best
> All things both great and small;
> For the dear God who loveth us,
> He made and loveth all.

The ultimate effect of a work of art depends only to a small degree on superficial complexities; and some of the immemorial simplicities of the fairy-tale stir our natures more fundamentally than the bright and rattling ingenuities of a good adventure story. Or one can point to the different areas of the mind which have interested the two modern psychologists who show the same kind of temperamental opposition as Plato and Aristotle among the Greeks, Jung and Freud. Jung did not deny the truth of much Freudian theorising about the mind but he thought it defective in leaving out those areas of the unconscious that mattered most: the primitive areas of instinctive wisdom accumulated through the ages by the collective efforts of the race. I do not either believe or disbelieve in the Jungian theory of the collective unconscious but I am clear in my own mind that in talking of it Jung points to certain basic mental possessions to which Freud and his kin are not very sensitive, and, further, that the poetry which appeals to those mental possessions has a special and at the same time wide-embracing power. I also think that the *Ancient Mariner* has that power, whereas the *Nocturnal upon St. Lucy's Day* has not. Since the power is wide-embracing, since it exists, even if usually dormant and unknown, in the minds of all men it implies a social sense: something I found missing in Donne's poem. In its restricted way Donne's *Nocturnal* is superb. But Coleridge in the *Ancient Mariner*, while being eminently himself, speaks for the whole of normal humanity and, so doing, creates a work of art of a different, and of a larger, dimension.

I have spent so long on Donne and Goldsmith and Coleridge that I may seem to have forgotten Milton and my initial comparison between the sonnets of Donne and Milton on their dead wives. But I have had my conclusion in mind; and it is that in this matter of the personal and the public Milton habitually comes between Goldsmith and Donne. There is personal poignancy in Samson's soliloquies unlike anything in Goldsmith:

> O that torment should not be confined
> To the body's wounds and sores
> With maladies innumerable
> In heart, head, breast, and reins;
> But must secret passage find
> To th'inmost mind,
> There exercise all his fierce accidents
> And on her purest spirits prey,
> As on entrails, joints, and limbs,
> With answerable pains, but more intense,
> Though void of corporal sense.
> My griefs not only pain me
> As a ling'ring disease,
> But finding no redress, ferment and rage
> Nor less than wounds immedicable
> Rankle and fester and gangrene,
> To black mortification.

But if this is personal beyond the scope of Goldsmith, there is a social aim in Milton's seeking to justify the ways of God to men in *Paradise Lost* unlike anything in Donne. Essentially Milton is closest to Coleridge in these matters. I do not wish to pursue this topic, having already written of Milton's social tone in my *Miltonic*

27

Setting; and I will end with quoting a relevant passage from that book occurring in the section on *L'Allegro* and *Il Penseroso*:

I fancy that *L'Allegro* and *Il Penseroso* are the most popular of Milton's poems because of their subtle friendliness of tone. Some poets deliberately exclude the reader's participation: these are the perversely obscure. Others, though admitting the reader, if he likes, to participate, do not invite. Others invite—Horace or Goldsmith. Others still, pester—Hugo and Whitman are apt to pester. Others again are coquettish: they pretend to be very aloof, but are really inviting very hard—a romantic vice, to be seen in Byron and the legion of the misunderstood. In *L'Allegro* and *Il Penseroso* Milton displays a perfect social tone. He reduces his idiosyncrasies to a minimum, without at all ceasing to be his characteristic self.

3

STRUCTURE

IN commenting on Donne's sonnet to his wife I noticed how the sequence of the poem turned in on itself.[1] His two opening sentiments proved after all superfluous because of a third sentiment. Not all Donne's poems are so extreme, though in a moment I will give a second example of such extremity. Nevertheless the sonnet illustrates a constant habit of Donne's mind, and one that applies, among the Metaphysicals, only to himself. It shows itself constantly in smaller or less complicated turns of thought. In *A Valediction: of Weeping* Donne first says that he and the lady are right to indulge in tears and sighs as the appropriate signs of valediction:

> Let me pour forth
> My tears before thy face—

but he goes back on the sentiment and begs the lady not to weep because, if she does, the winds and waves he encounters on his journey will be stimulated to sympathy and will drown him. In *Good Friday riding westward* Donne says he ought to be riding east towards

---

[1] I can imagine a critic saying: 'You make too much of this habit, which is simply the rhetorical device of *epanorthosis*, well known in Donne's day and hence not surprising'. I retort: 'This makes no difference. Donne and his age had rhetoric in their minds all the time. What matters is the choice of rhetorical devices and the uses to which they are put.'

Jerusalem but he is not; he is riding westward. He can do the same thing in a single line, as in the opening of one of the greatest religious sonnets, 'At the round earth's imagined corners . . .', which contains the thought that there should be corners of the earth because the Bible refers to them but there are not because science has demonstrated that the world is round. In fact the characteristic movement of Donne's mind is summed up in the statement: *it is, but it isn't after all.* Or, to be more explicit, I will quote Helen Gardner's pronouncement from the introduction to her recent edition of the Divine Poems:

> Donne was a man of strong passions in whom an appetite for life was crossed by a strong distaste for it. He is satirist and elegist at the same period, and even in the same poem. The scorn of the satirist invades the world of amorous elegy; his gayest poems have a note of bitterness; his most passionate poems are rarely free from a note of contempt.[1]

And now let me reinforce my argument by pointing to a poem, most typical of Donne, that has just the structure of his sonnet to his dead wife. Grierson includes it in his anthology of Metaphysical poetry but I am not convinced it is worth that distinction, for the feeling displayed hardly equals the ingenuity. It is *Lovers' Infiniteness.* There are three verses and they concern the scholastic question whether or not the poet can possess all the love of his mistress, with the initial

[1] *Donne, the Divine Poems* (Oxford, 1952) xxxv.

implication that it would be a good thing if he could. The first verse and most of the second argue that he can't have all his mistress's love; and he gives several ingenious reasons. He is bankrupt of sighs tears and letters, the usual purchase-money of love. Nor is his mistress in *his* debt, because she did not bargain to give more than the quantity she agreed on when they became lovers. And he is not certain that even then she gave him all she had; she may have kept some for others. Then Donne makes his first turn—perhaps she did give him all then—only to reverse it; for what ultimate difference does that make, when fresh love may have grown in her heart *since* this total gift, and others may have got it:

> Or if then thou gavest me all,
> 'All' was but all which thou hadst then.
> But if in thy heart, since, there be or shall
> New love created be by other men
> (Which have their stocks entire and can in tears,
> In sighs, in oaths, and letters outbid me)
> This new love may beget new fears,
> For this love was not vowed by thee.

And then, in the last three lines of the second verse he turns right back on all he has said and asserts that he possesses the freehold of his mistress's heart and that all the love that grows belongs to him as landlord and can't be given away. But that is not all. Abruptly, in the third verse he destroys the whole structure, every crookedness included, by going back on the supposition underlying it: namely that he *wants* to enjoy all his mistress's love. He now finds that he doesn't and that he prefers to have it in instalments. And he ends with still one more turn: the best solution is to finish with giving and receiving altogether; and that can be done by amalgamating the two hearts into one. Like the ending of the *Good Morrow* this one is feeble and perfunctory, a nominal and inorganic piece of finality, the truth being that the poem exists for no *end* whatever; the journey is everything, the arrival nothing. The poet in fact presents us with a number of conflicting options; and the point is that the options *should* conflict and that no choice should be made. Being fascinated by the processes of thought and having no faith in thought's leading anywhere he watches masochistically its painful convolutions. He enjoys throwing a spanner into his own mental machine and watching what happens, or, if you like, he agonises over the invisible ground he stands on, refusing to go forward.

In other argumentative poets you may find an interest in the journey and in the processes of thought, but it is never as in Donne the main thing. Lucretius enjoyed arguing but he strove to reach conclusions. The words he loves and pronounces passionately are the *wherefores* and the *therefores*: *hinc, igitur, quare, quapropter, quare etiam atque etiam.* These are words about which Donne feels the most coolly. To illustrate the norm of the English Metaphysicals in this matter I choose a poem that superficially has some resemblance to Donne in its preference for the journey over the destination: it is Marvell's *The Mower to the Glow-*

worms. And I shall seek to show that beneath the surface it is very different from anything of Donne's.

> Ye living lamps, by whose dear light
>   The nightingale does sit so late,
> And studying all the summer night
>   Her matchless songs does meditate;
>
> Ye country comets, that portend
>   No war nor prince's funeral,
> Shining unto no higher end
>   Than to presage the grass's fall;
>
> Ye glow-worms, whose officious flame
>   To wandering mowers shows the way,
> That in the night have lost their aim,
>   And after foolish fires do stray;
>
> Your courteous lights in vain you waste,
>   Since Juliana here is come;
> For she my mind hath so displaced,
>   That I shall never find my home.

Here the last verse has the same office as some of Donne's endings: it is a perfunctory and not at all serious valediction. Indeed Marvell's Juliana is a mere convenience for pulling the shape of the poem together; more like a corset than a living woman. The interest lies in the varied and amazing purposes the poet fancies the glow-worms to serve. These begin as the candles by whose light the nightingale reads the tune of his air in the song-book. They go on to be miniature rustic comets portending the catastrophic fall of the grass; but in so doing they switch the reader suddenly from the wildest fantasy to the soberest fact, for it is quite true that the glow-worms haunt the long grass as it ripens for harvest. Then they become kindly beacons or lighthouses that put back on the true road the late reapers, agents of their prognostication, who have been led astray by will-o'-the-wisps. And this kindly function leads to the final thought that with all their good intentions they can't help the poet, whose mind has been distracted by Juliana beyond repair.

There are two main ways in which Marvell differs radically from Donne. Both poems are complicated; but while Donne's complication has to do with the processes of his thought, Marvell's has to do with the imaginative ingenuity of his comparisons. Marvell varies a single theme; Donne keeps on crossing one theme by another. Secondly, although Marvell does not complicate the processes of thought like Donne, the thought-content of his poem is exceedingly rich. The connotations of Donne's thought are few, its ramifications insignificant; when the thought-processes have been enjoyed (and they can supply keen enjoyment) interest ceases. But Marvell's thought is full of suggestion. The touch of reality in the second verse brings another area of the mind into play. With the hint of real cosmic prodigies and high political events the miniature activity of the glow-worms is given an august setting and at the same time becomes laughable. We should see these insects in their cosmic setting, in their proper place in the chain of being, performing their miniature function as glow-worms with exemplary zest, and not the less praiseworthy because they become comic through the small size of their allowed activity. Further, the stale Petrarchian conceit of the last verse gives the mind a jolt after the fresh and skittish fantasy of the first three verses. Marvell's poem, in fact, has for its theme the spice of life, the spice of its variety, of its mixture of the large and the small, the solemn and the humorous, the spice that makes it sweet to the man of discriminating appetite. Feeling certain of his subject Marvell is content to plot his poem simply. He varies and he weights his theme; but he has no need to turn on himself, to find that after all he must say the opposite of what he began with. He is not contorted, but, safe in the richness of his thought and feeling, he has no occasion to shun a fundamental simplicity.

But this matter of structure can point to some larger general considerations which I touched on in my prefatory remarks on the two sonnets of Donne and Milton: the comparative closeness of different kinds of poetry to the sphere of action. From what I have already said it is plain that Marvell, with his greater regard for ends, is nearer to action than Donne is. But I may make myself clearer if I point to a kind of poetry that is nearer still.

In his writings on the theory of literature I. A. Richards makes much of the importance of 'attitudes': that is 'attitudes' in their technical, psychological sense of impulses towards action which end not in action itself but in a substituted readiness to act. These 'attitudes' are like the point in a high-class game of chess when the two opponents see that one has gained a slight advantage over the other bringing the virtual certainty of a win for one of them; whereupon they cease action and substitute for it admissions of victory on the one hand and of defeat on the other. With Richards's further theory that in the modern world attitudes are destined to oust action and that hence poetry, which deals with attitudes, has a glorious future I am not concerned, though I cannot forbear saying by the way that I much doubt whether in the kind of world he describes men would *want* to make use of the opportunities for poetry lavished on them; hence that I do not share his optimism. My present point is that I agree to poetry's having *some* relation to deeds. Up to a certain point the impulse behind great poetry and great deeds is the same, even if there comes the point where the choice has to be made between the immediate practical effect and the fixed symbolic substitute whose very fixity sacrifices the immediate effect to the future potentiality. Shelley went further than this and said in his *Defence of Poetry*:

> Poets . . . are not only the authors of language and of music, of the dance, and architecture, and statuary, and painting: they are the institutors of laws, and the founders of civil society, and the inventors of the arts of life, and the teachers who draw into a certain propinquity with the beautiful and the true that partial apprehension of the agencies of the invisible world which is called

religion. . . . Poets, according to the circumstances of the age and nation in which they appeared, were called, in the earlier epochs of the world, legislators or prophets; a poet essentially comprises and unites both these characters.

Again, I am not concerned with the precise truth of this position; but, instead, I suggest that different kinds of poetry are at different removes from the region of deeds. I am not thinking of the difference between, for instance, drama and the lyric, between literature that presents deeds and literature that does not; I am thinking of the state of mind prompting or pervading the work of art. In his interesting essay *On Metaphysical Poetry* [1] James Smith notes how the last lines of Donne's *The Good Morrow*, into which the poem is supposed to issue, scarcely exist, the poem being virtually over before them. Now that is typical. Donne is interested in definitions, analyses, and suppositions; he is little interested in the things into which they issue, even if in his sermons he forced himself against his natural inclinations. Shelley, on the other hand, as one would expect from the passage I read from the *Defence of Poetry*, is temperamentally the exact opposite. For all his lyrical gift he remained in his poetry the man with a passion for reforming the world. That passion led him to deeds as well as words: to trying to raise money in London to repair a breakwater in a distant Welsh town as well as to composing the *Revolt of Islam*.

It may be helpful here to consider for a moment

[1] In *Determinations*, ed. F. R. Leavis (London, 1934).

the family backgrounds of the two poets. Donne, in his preface to *Biathanatos*, has described his own:

> I had my first breeding and conversation with men of suppressed and afflicted religion, accustomed to the despite of death and hungry of an imagined martyrdom.

It was a background where men were thrown in on themselves, where action consisted of subterfuge and resistance, and where doubt mingled with heroism. There was nothing forthright about it. Shelley was born into a family which found life simple. A squire in the eighteenth century knew what was expected of him and had answers ready-made to meet the contingencies of life. He knew his station and the occupations appropriate to it. Now both Donne and Shelley had the original sort of temperament that is unlikely to accept the assumptions current in their early surroundings. Whether or not such people rebel actively depends on how tactfully their families handle them; but, rebellion or no rebellion, they will be certain to question the code they are born into, very thoroughly. Donne did not rebel against the paternal religion but he questioned its claims to absolute truth and he ended by leaving it. And there may have been some defiance in the licentious life we imagine him to have led as a young man. But whatever the questionings or the defiance amount to, Donne's *poetical* quality matches his family background singularly well. Men in opposition and liable to persecution are not usually strong in a general social sense; while the active sides of their nature are denied a forthright issue into action and are turned back on themselves. Shelley, mishandled by a stupid father, maltreated at school, and again mishandled at college, became a rebel in spite of his naturally forthcoming and affectionate heart. Nevertheless, he retained the masterful, energetic, and forthright disposition of an English squire of the eighteenth century; and in most of his poetry he has no more doubt of what he is after than Sir Timothy Shelley and his like riding to hounds.

Most of Shelley's poetry is quite exceptionally close to action. It is versified preaching with certain very clear, if unattainable, ends. To Shelley, for much of his life, they were not only clear but attainable. This closeness to action is at once Shelley's strength and weakness. He is like a greyhound on the dog-track. The vision of the electric hare incites him to prodigious effort. But he mistakes the electric hare for a real one; and the technique of his racing inclines to be repetitive. Thus he does not make the fullest use of the extraordinary powers at his disposal. I conjecture that the *Revolt of Islam* is the greatest waste of sheer poetical talent in our language. It is of the length of a small epic, nearly five thousand lines; it is in the difficult Spenserian stanza; and it keeps its energy to the end. It also abounds in fine passages, in passages of nearly but hardly ever quite the best poetry. Yet even when Shelley's reputation was at its height, not his warmest admirers took the whole of the *Revolt of Islam* to their hearts. In many ways it is a most touching poem: a poem founded on the belief that love is more powerful than hate and that it is possible at any time in the world's history for love to take the initiative and to achieve a revolution. What is wrong with the world is that men of good will lack courage, fail to know their strength, and will not act. And when Shelley rises to a prophetic vein in preaching his gospel he can speak with a compelling emphasis or achieve a most impetuous speed. Here is a passage describing the nature of love and its suppression by a foolish and unthinking obedience (Canto VIII, stanzas 11-13):

> O Love, who to the hearts of wandering men
> Art as the calm to Ocean's weary waves!
> Justice, or Truth, or Joy! those only can
> From slavery and religion's labyrinth caves
> Guide us, as one clear star the seaman saves.
> To give to all an equal share of good,
> To track the steps of Freedom, though through
>   graves
> She pass, to suffer all in patient mood,
> To weep for crime, though stained with thy friend's
>   dearest blood,—
>
> To feel the peace of self-contentment's lot,
> To own all sympathies and outrage none,
> Or in the inmost bowers of sense and thought,
> Until life's sunny day is quite gone down,
> To sit and smile with Joy, or, not alone,
> To kiss salt tears from the worn cheek of Woe;
> To live, as if to love and live were one,—
> This is not faith or law, nor those who bow
> To thrones on Heaven or Earth, such destiny may
>   know.

But children near their parents tremble now,
Because they must obey—one rules another,
And as one Power rules both high and low,
So man is made the captive of his brother,
And Hate is throned on high with Fear her mother,
Above the Highest—and those fountain-cells,
 Whence love yet flowed when faith had choked all
  other,
 Are darkened—Woman as the bond-slave dwells
Of man, a slave; and life is poisoned in its wells.

The whole tenour is that of urgency. Awake, awake,
the world is stifled with evil deeds, with the lethargy
of custom, with the oppression of kings and priests.
But it need not be. The spirit of man is not to be
quenched, love remains, though driven underground
or into corners, and will enjoy its destined spring.

The blasts of Autumn drive the wingèd seeds
Over the earth,—next come the snows, and rain,
And frosts, and storms, which dreary Winter leads
Out of his Scythian cave, a savage train;
Behold! Spring sweeps over the world again,
Shedding soft dews from her ethereal wings;
Flowers on the mountains, fruits over the plain,
And music on the waves and woods she flings,
 And love on all that lives, and calm on lifeless things.[1]

It was unthinkable for Shelley to turn back on himself,
to question or to hesitate. Nothing but the fierce pursuit
of his goal was possible; anything less would be to
betray his trust.

[1] IX. 21.

Observe also that in these stanzas Shelley has been giving his version of winter as Donne gave it in his *Nocturnal*. But how different a winter! For Donne the depths of winter symbolise the depths of negation to which his own spirit has fallen; for Shelley they symbolise the *social* degradation of man. And in those depths lie the seeds of renewal and resurrection for all humanity. If, as the French habitually do, we should use the words *classical* and *romantic* in the sense of *social* and *individual* respectively, we shall see that Shelley is not a romantic at all but, for all his rebellion, the faithful heir of the social conscience of the eighteenth century.

I have spoken of Donne and Marvell and Shelley. What of Milton? Does he plot his poems after the manner of one of these, or has he his own method? It is pretty well agreed that among Milton's longer lyrics the *Nativity Ode* approaches in its manner nearest to the Metaphysicals; and I will use it to illustrate my answer. A reason for this approximation is the number of ingenious and fanciful comparisons that Milton introduces. These, however, are not at all like the contortions of Donne and are very much like the richly suggestive fantasies I found in Marvell. I need go no further than the two opening stanzas of the hymn for an illustration:

It was the winter wild,
While the heav'n-born child
    All meanly wrapp'd in the rude manger lies;
Nature in awe to him

Had doff'd her gaudy trim,
    With her great master so to sympathize:
It was no season then for her
To wanton with the sun, her lusty paramour.

Only with speeches fair
She wooes the gentle air
    To hide her guilty front with innocent snow,
And on her naked shame,
Pollute with sinful blame,
    The saintly veil of maiden white to throw,
Confounded that her maker's eyes
Should look so near upon her foul deformities.

Now there was a tradition, going back to Plato, that
the earth was a living creature. But in the gay and
delicate fantasy of the earth, alienated for the moment
from her lover the sun and trying to persuade the air
to hide her imperfections with snow, I do not think
there is any reference to this strange and solemn doc-
trine. Milton turning the earth into a living creature,
of female sex, indulges in make-believe quite as much
as Marvell turning two glow-worms into a couple of
candles flanking a desk to light the score of a song-book
for the benefit of a nightingale. Nevertheless the fantasy
is serious as illustrating a truth. Milton believed that
human life on earth was sinful and that at the season
of the year when the redeemer of earthly sin was about
to arrive a posture of penance was fitter than the passion
of love. Moreover, he knew that in the Christian year
Advent was a season of fast. Like Marvell's, Milton's
thought is rich. Unlike Donne he is not concerned with

any complication of the processes of thought. That is, not in the act of expressing himself in these opening stanzas. Later in the poem, as in *Lycidas*, he does actually resemble Donne in going back on himself: for there he pictures the golden age that comes in with the birth of Christ; only to add that this can't be so after all.

> But wisest fate says no,
> This must not yet be so,
>   The babe lies yet in smiling infancy,
> That on the bitter cross
> Must redeem our loss;
>   So both himself and us to glorify:
> Yet first to those ychain'd in sleep
> The wakeful trump of doom must
>   thunder through the deep.

And the poem, having dallied with the Golden Age and shot forward to the Last Day, retracts and settles to the final theme, the present happiness that the birth of Christ confers. And this theme had never been lost from view.

In *Lycidas* Milton goes back on his epitaphic theme to inveigh against the corrupt clergy of his day and to toy with the fancy that Lycidas is not dead at all but that somewhere past the Hebrides, like a fabulous character in the *Faerie Queene*, he visits the bottom of the monstrous world or is asleep on the Cornish coast by St. Michael's shrine,

> Where the great vision of the guarded mount
> Looks toward Namancos and Bayona's hold.

But in neither poem is Milton's turning back on himself more than a temporary enrichment of his theme. He uses his turns and his second thoughts to make his journey interesting, but he never forgets his destination. The course of *Lycidas* is wonderful, enchanting, and terrifying by turns, but Milton has been working all the time towards the solution of the theme, the apotheosis of Lycidas and the spiritual lesson it conveys. And the last two lines with their suggestion of novelty and the symbolic reference to hope in the blue [1] of the shepherd's mantle—

> At last he rose and twitch'd his mantle blue:
> Tomorrow to fresh woods and pastures new—

show the questing type of mind Milton possessed, a mind the very opposite of the one that fails to reach conclusions and is most involved in the processes of its thought.

Yet Milton is more reflective than Shelley. In the end he occupies a middle position with Marvell.

[1] See R. C. Fox in the *Explicator*, June 1951.

4

RHETORIC

WHY is it that those who write about Donne make so much of the novelty of his fitting his verse to the pressure and the undulations of the speaking voice, when other poets had already succeeded in this matter, and when the very matter itself has constituted one of the prime problems of literary creation throughout the ages?

If any rhetorical facts are plain, then it is plain first that there must always be some difference between the rhythms and the diction of verse and of vulgar speech, and secondly that the two must be related and that this relation must constantly fluctuate. It is true further that literature can be renewed and refreshed by altering that relation: a much sounder assertion than that literature ought, or ought not, to be near to, or far from, the spoken language. The present point will be whether Donne and no one else to the same degree did in fact alter this relation.

It is perfectly possible to argue that Donne was anything but a pioneer in approximating poetry to the spoken word in a non-dramatic literary medium. Chaucer, for instance, was master of the effect in many places, and conspicuously in the end-links of the *Canterbury Tales*. I do not see how anything in this mode could be better than these words of the host to the

Reeve after the Miller has told his tale:

> Whan that oure Host hadde herd this sermonyng,
> He gan to speke as lordly as a kyng.
> He seide, 'What amounteth al this wit?
> What, shul we speke alday of hooly writ?
> The devel made a reve for to preche,
> Or of a soutere a shipman or a leche.
> Sey forth thy tale, and tarie not the tyme.
> Lo Depeford! and it is half-wey pryme.
> Lo Grenewych, ther many a shrewe is inne!
> It were al tyme thy tale to begynne.'

On all these lines there is the pressure of the spoken word. It would be possible to argue further that all through English literature the art of maintaining that pressure has been practised, independently of any possible influence from Donne. Prior, early in the eighteenth century, wrote to his Cloe, jealous :

> Dear Cloe, how blubber'd is that pretty face!
>   Thy cheek all on fire, and thy hair all uncurl'd.
> Prithee, quit this caprice; and, as old Falstaff says,
>   Let us e'en talk a little like folks of this world.
>
> How canst thou presume, thou hast leave to destroy
>   The beauties which Venus but lent to thy keeping?
> Those looks were design'd to inspire love and joy:
>   More ord'nary eyes may serve people for weeping.
>
> To be vex'd at a trifle or two that I writ
>   Your judgement at once and my passion you wrong:
> You take that for fact which will scarce be found wit;
>   Od's life! must one swear to the truth of a song?

.   .   .   .   .

Then finish, dear Cloe, this pastoral war;
  And let us like Horace and Lydia agree:
For thou art a girl as much brighter than her
  As he was a poet sublimer than me.

Here the words are familiar, the word-order of speech
hardly altered, and the emphases much those we make
in animated conversation. Or take two verses from a
more recent ballad:

'You are old, Father William', the young man said,
  'And your hair has become very white;
And yet you incessantly stand on your head—
  Do you think, at your age, it is right?'
'In my youth', Father William replied to his son,
  'I feared it might injure the brain;
But, now that I'm perfectly sure I have none,
  Why, I do it again and again.'

If you retort, as indeed you can, that the two poems
in question are not in the main stream of contemporary
literary creation, I can point to Wyatt and say that not
only was he in the main stream of lyric creation but
that he came before Donne in letting the drama into
lyric verse and making it talk. Take this example
(*bourds* means *mockery*):

Madame, withouten many words,
  Once, I am sure, ye will or no:
And, if ye will, then leave your bourds
  And use your wit, and shew it so;

And with a beck ye shall me call.
  And if of one that burneth alway

48

Ye have any pity at all,
   Answer him fair with yea or nay.
If it be yea, I shall be fain;
   If it be nay, friends as before;
Ye shall another man obtain,
   And I mine own and yours no more.

In 1541 Wyatt was in prison, a victim of the suspicions of Henry VIII. While there he wrote an octave to his friend Sir Francis Brian describing his fate and his feelings. It is a much more passionate affair than the little love lyric, but it resembles Donne in the sense it gives of the speaking voice, of a voice expressing grief almost intolerable but gradually mastered. Note how the first line anticipates in its rhythm the famous opening of Donne's *Twicknam Garden*, 'Blasted with sighs and surrounded with tears'.

Sighs are my food, drink are my tears
(Clinking of fetters such music would crave);
Stink and close air away my life wears;
Innocency is all the hope I have.
Rain wind or weather I judge by mine ears.
Malice assaulted that righteousness should have.
Sure I am, Brian, this wound shall heal again,
But yet, alas, the scar shall still remain.

On the face of it you would say that Wyatt had done for English lyric verse (albeit on a smaller scale) just what Donne was to do. Where, then, is the credit due? The answer is that the question is not one of credit but of effect. Donne was the greater man and though he may have done the same thing as Wyatt he did it at a

49

more opportune time. Wyatt lived at a time when the forces of creation were slack. There was no eager body of followers to welcome him, to encourage him through its welcome to redouble his efforts, and to carry on, adapt, and develop what he had begun. Wyatt was popular but not more than his junior, Surrey, whose lyrical manner was smooth and conventional, and far from the conversational mode of his predecessor. And though the mode of Wyatt did not quite drop, that of Surrey represented better the trend the age of Elizabeth was destined to favour. You will find passages in Sidney's lyrics that show the pressure of the speaking voice, but he launched no general revolution nor does he visibly continue the Wyatt tradition. When Donne was impelled to do what Wyatt did, he had to begin again from the beginning.[1] And, though I have just said that the matter of credit is irrelevant, I am impelled to add here that any credit that is due belongs to each poet alike.

In claiming that Donne had to do the work of Wyatt over again I may offend those who think that Donne's originality has been exaggerated. That his originality of *substance* was exaggerated in the first days of revived enthusiasm is certain. Then, people knew less about medieval science and school-learning and were ready enough to agree with Carew when, in his elegy on Donne, he praised him for having abandoned the conventional Anacreontic and Ovidian material and

[1] I speak only of the lyric. The influence of Chapman and the beginnings of the impulse towards satire may have a rather different tale to tell.

'fresh invention planted'. Carew had not been brought
up a Catholic and may have forgotten or not have
read Paracelsus and other learned writers. Anyhow he
ignored the derivative nature of Donne's scholastic
and scientific lore and sited his 'fresh invention' in the
wrong place. Mario Praz has been one of the pioneers
in exploding the misplaced notion of Donne's originality and in showing that he was not less indebted than
his poetic contemporaries, though it was a different debt.

Well, whatever the degree of Donne's originality, its
nature is not of substance but of rhetoric. And the
rhetorical innovations he introduced into the lyric were
timed more happily than the similar innovations of
Wyatt. The language of the drama was changing; and
that change was preparing people for what Donne was
impelled to do. Wyatt lacked any such advantage.
Nor do I think that it is fair to belittle Donne's credit
on account of this parallel dramatic development or that
we should agree entirely with Coleridge when he wrote:

> After all there is but one Donne! but now tell me yet,
> wherein, in *his own kind*, he differs from the similar power
> in Shakespeare? Shakespeare was all men, potentially,
> except Milton.

In a way Coleridge is right. You can find somewhere
in Shakespeare's plays a good proportion of the feelings
Donne exploited. But it is one thing to put certain
feelings into a play, another to put them into a lyric.
And, allow all you will for Donne's material being
derivative, rob the state of ecstasy and the image of

the compasses of all surprise and reduce them to contemporary commonplace; yet you do not at all change
the hard fact that Donne wrought a revolution in
the English lyric, a revolution best put in terms of the
technique of poetry. He extended the tempo, and he
enriched the rhythms of the English lyric: and he did
these things partly by approximating its rhetoric to
that of the vulgar tongue; and so thoroughly that he
diverted no negligible part of the current of English
verse into the rhetorical channel he dug.

This achievement can be separated from the personal
idiosyncrasies I described in my last section: Donne's
'subtlety to plague himself' and his reluctance to reach
a destination. Donne's so-called Metaphysical followers
did not share these. Herbert or Carew or Vaughan
are in these matters like the least Metaphysical poets
of the age, Waller or Herrick, and quite alien to Donne:
they know where they want to go and they are interested in arriving. But Donne's expansion of lyrical
rhetoric helped many poets, and may have stimulated
indirectly some who superficially owe nothing to him.
In fact Donne's special revolution may have helped
the general sharpening of tone that makes the standard
of lyrical writing in the first half of the seventeenth
century so astonishingly high. Herrick, whose sharp
edge is now better recognised thanks to the efforts of
S. Musgrove and Cleanth Brooks among others, though
he owes nothing directly to Donne, either in substance
or rhythm, may have drawn strength from the general
sense of urgency, of present actuality, that Donne

helped to give to the lyrical tradition in England.

I will reinforce this sentiment about Herrick by illustrating from one of his best known poems. And I do this because one of my objects in these lectures is, except for Donne, to seek to approximate the different poets and to continue the process, already begun, of breaking down their departmentalisation into schools. Not that they did not have very marked individuality, but the individuality is attached not to separate schools of poets but to a general temper that marks the age. The poem is *To the Virgins, to make much of Time*:

> Gather ye rosebuds, while ye may,
>   Old Time is still a-flying;
> And this same flower that smiles today
>   Tomorrow will be dying.
>
> The glorious lamp of heaven, the sun,
>   The higher he's a-getting,
> The sooner will his race be run,
>   The nearer he's to setting.
>
> That age is best which is the first,
>   When youth and blood are warmer;
> But being spent, the worse, and worst
>   Times still succeed the former.
>
> Then be not coy but use your time,
>   And while ye may go marry:
> For having lost but once your prime
>   You may for ever tarry.

In almost every way the poem seems to violate the example of Donne. The thought presses on to the end without pause or turn. There is a quietist or Epicurean acceptance of the conditions of life in it and no subtle contrivance for self-torture. Carew in his elegy on Donne stated pessimistically that Donne's revolutionary act of getting free from the imitation of classical commonplaces would not last, being too hard a feat for smaller men:

> But thou art gone, and thy strict laws will be
> Too hard for libertines in poetry.
> They will repeal the goodly exil'd train
> Of gods and goddesses, which in thy just reign
> Were banish'd nobler poems.

And he laments that Donne's rhythms will degenerate into ballad time and that the old idols will be adored again with new apostasy. Herrick perfectly fulfils Carew's pessimism. The sentiment of his poem is classical in origin. The 'glorious lamp of heaven, the sun' is certainly Phoebus Apollo. The metre is the swift-running ballad metre. The only possible resemblance with Donne would be in the simple language. But it was Ben Jonson, if anyone, who taught Herrick his special brand of simplicity. And yet his lines make their impression, they succeed somehow in adhering to the brain—except perhaps to the brains of those who have been carefully schooled to think such simplicities are contemptible and have thus been conditioned out of their natural responses. And, in actual fact, the lines are far from simple; and it is precisely their artful complexity that both captivates us and makes them so firm a part of their age.

The trend of the poem is urgency touched with reflection. There is a touch of reflection in 'old Time', for he is more than the personified *vieillard* with scythe and hour-glass, *old* meaning not only *aged* but *recurrent*, the recurrent ill, the 'blight man was born for'. Through the word the poet informs us that he knows he is treating once again the immemorial theme. But more than half the poem has to do with the urgency, with the need for present action. And it is not only the verse that hurries us along; the thought co-operates to make the sense of urgency convincing. The bud becomes a flower; today gives way to tomorrow; and heaped up comparative adjectives—higher, sooner, nearer, warmer, worse—move towards the superlative and the inevitable dwindling that follows it. The rhythm of the third verse brilliantly suggests the dwindling process. The voice is forced to pause on 'worst times'; if it doesn't it confounds the two words. And the speed of 'still succeed the former' is that of descent not of exaltation. In fact the rhythm of the verse suggests the rapid momentum up a slope on a switch-back railway, the pause on the top (*worst times*) as the vehicle just succeeds in making the crest, and the falling away on the other side of the slope. Reflection ensues in the first line of the last verse, with the conclusive *then* (compare what I said of Lucretius's *quare's* and *quapropter's*) and in the bold emphasis on *use*. The rest of the verse slips away in harmony with the prevailing hurry.

Now all the details co-operate in persuading us that Herrick has really something to say in spite of the measureless triteness of the sentiment. If I were pressed to enlarge on this something, I should proceed on these lines. It is plain that any value the poem has resides not in the sentiment but in what the poet makes of it. And what he makes of it may become clearer if we inquire what other poets have made of the same sentiment. I think of a few lines from Webster's *Duchess of Malfi* where the same sentiment occurs but with a very different effect. Duke Ferdinand has been trying to bully his sister the Duchess into forswearing marriage. The Duchess retorts and ends with the words:

> Why should only I,
> Of all the other princes of the world,
> Be cas'd up like a holy relic? I have youth
> And a little beauty.

If Herrick in his caption tells the virgins to make much of time, the young widow in Webster's play gives herself the same advice; but no one could pretend that the connotations of this common advice are at all similar. Webster by bringing in religion through the words 'holy relic' and stressing the word *little* arouses solemn feelings and strikes an acute contrast. There is something defiant in the way his Duchess insists on her small rights in the mighty setting; or if you are sceptical of the religious implications, at least, you must agree, she makes it clear that beauty and pleasure, however insistent in their claims, are short and evanescent compared with the ills of life. We know that trouble and conflict are bound to follow the assertion of her will.

Herrick is not subject to any such pessimism. 'There is a tragic element in life' he seems to say through the alert yet resigned flow of his stanzas, 'yet life is not too bad if you know its terms. Make the best of it and don't worry overmuch. The worse times are coming, but why let them spoil the present? Eat your grapes downwards.[1] Sufficient unto the day is the evil thereof.' This is a definite way of thinking about life. It may not be the best but it has its value. It is unambitious but it may promote good or even fine living within limits. And it is for such fine living that this and other of Herrick's poems stand. To stray for a moment outside the frontiers of legitimate criticism, I like to imagine that Herrick himself lived up to his philosophy. Confined for most of his days to a kind of country life not quite to his taste (he did not, like Herbert, have a cathedral town within easy walking distance) he seems to have set himself to making the best of things and to have gathered the joys within his reach, stifling his desires for those beyond it. In this spirit he fancied that his Devonshire village was in pagan Greece or amused himself in writing an epitaph on his house-keeper before she died or in training one of his pigs to drink beer out of a tankard. In all he was courageous, serene, religious up to a point, and full, in spite of the limits ordained him, of the zest for life.

I remarked, before pointing to a single poem of Herrick's, that Donne may have had the general effect

---

[1] Samuel Butler's phrase. See his section, 'Eating Grapes Downwards', in *Note-Books*, 99.

of sharpening the tone of lyrical writing. But I do not wish to deny his special effect on certain poets, or rather on certain poems of certain poets. Donne's direct influence on Herbert was undoubted but it extended to a smaller proportion of his poems than is often thought. It did extend to some of the best. The lovely conversational tone of the *Church Floor*, for instance, cooler and less turbulent in its effect than Donne, is certainly derived from him. The drama of the vicar showing his friend the church is exquisitely conveyed, without the least vulgarity or ostentation; and, though its virtues are Herbert's, its mode goes back to Donne.

> Mark you the floor? that square and speckled stone,
> Which looks so firm and strong,
>   Is Patience.
> And th' other black and grave, wherewith each one
> Is checker'd all along,
>   Humility.
> The gentle rising, which on either hand
> Leads to the choir above,
>   Is Confidence.
> But the sweet cement, which in one sure band
> Ties the whole frame, is Love
>   And Charity.

Vaughan imitated Donne directly in two of his secular poems and in a few of his religious ones he continues, whether through Herbert or not, the air of thinking aloud, for instance in *Distraction*:

> O knit me, that am crumbled dust! the heap
> Is all dispers'd and cheap;

RHETORIC

Give for a handful but a thought
And it is bought.

Hadst thou
Made me a star, a pearl, or a rainbow,
The beams I then had shot
My light had lessen'd not;
But now
I find myself the less the more I grow.

And one could make quite a compilation of Donne-
imitations from the minor poets. Here is one from
Patrick Carey (included in Saintsbury *Caroline Poets*)
which I give to show to what depths the example of
Donne can lead, if the spirit is lacking:

For God's sake, mark that fly:
See what a poor, weak, little thing it is.
When thou hast mark'd, and scorn'd it, know
    that this,
This little, poor weak fly
Has kill'd a pope; can make an emp'ror die.

Behold yon spark of fire:
How little hot, how near to nothing 'tis.
When thou hast done despising, know that this,
This contemn'd spark of fire,
Has burnt whole towns; can burn a world entire.

That crawling worm there see:
Ponder how ugly, filthy, vile it is.
When thou hast seen and loathed it, know that this,
This base worm thou dost see,
Has quite devoured thy parents; shall eat thee.

Honour, the world, and man,
What trifles are they; since most true it is
That this poor fly, this little spark, this
So much abhorr'd worm, can
Honour destroy; burn worlds; devour up man.

But poets must not be held responsible for the short-comings of their admirers and imitators. Donne's domestication of the fluctuating rhythms of speech in the English lyric was one of the great positive innovations. Future opinion may turn the other way, from the rhythms of speech to rhetorical artifice; but it would be a crime if that innovation were ever allowed, as it once was, to be slighted and neglected. It ought to keep a permanent place in our literary consciousness, whether or not the time remains propitious for its immediate effect on the poetic production of the day.

I add no Miltonic comparison here, because my next section, on Milton and his relation to the Metaphysicals generally, includes some remarks on the rhetoric of his verse.

5

MILTON

EXCEPT possibly in the first of his two poems on Hobson, Milton does not introduce into his verse the rhythms of familiar speech. He can be genuinely dramatic in *Comus*, in the Devils' debate in *Paradise Lost* he can give the sense of parliamentary rhetoric, and in the temptation scene in the same poem he can make us feel that the characters are really conversing. But, strangely enough, it is in *Paradise Regained* that we get passages that can compare with the Hobson poem in suggesting the ordinary speaking voice. This is Satan telling Christ of his present relations with mankind:

> Men, generally, think me much a foe
> To all mankind: why should I? they to me
> Never did wrong or violence; by them
> I lost not what I lost, rather by them
> I gain'd what I have gain'd, and with them dwell
> Copartner in these regions of the world,
> If not disposer; lend them oft my aid,
> Oft my advice by presages and signs,
> And answers, oracles, portents and dreams,
> Whereby they may direct their future life.

Here the natural pauses, the slow tempo, the simple words, the sinuous progress suggest the ordinary conversation of an accomplished, highly educated man. But the nature of the passage is related not to the innovations of Donne but rather to those of the Restoration, when the prose of drama and of didacticism began to be purged of its roughnesses and to seek its criteria in the best talk of the best educated type of courtier. One can eliminate the whole of that side of Donne's influence.

On the other hand, Milton shared and benefited by the astringency and the athleticism that generally marked the early seventeenth century. One of the best accounts of the general character of the age (an account whose excellence consists not in any novelty but in the superior way the old truths are put) is in Basil Willey's *Seventeenth Century Background*. It is a pity that he applies it to the Metaphysicals, for it holds good for the whole age; for Herrick as much as for Herbert. Willey describes the current skill in living in distinguished worlds and in being able to pass deftly from one to another. He then describes these worlds:

> Many different worlds or countries of the mind then lay close together—the world of scholastic learning, the world of scientific experiment, the worlds of classical mythology and of biblical history, of fable and of fact, of theology and demonology, of sacred and profane love, of pagan and christian morals, of activity and contemplation; and a cultivated man had the freedom of them all. They were divided and distinguished, perhaps, but not, as later, by such high barriers that a man was shut up for life in one or other of them. The distinctions were only beginning to be made which for later years shut off poetry from science, metaphor from fact, fancy from judgment.

These sentences describe successfully how the writers of a whole age differed not only from subsequent ages of specialisation but from Lydgate and the authors of *Gorboduc*, those laborious explorers of single tracks over a long distance.

When Willey goes on to say that the Metaphysical mind is marked by its refusal to be finally committed to any one world, I doubt if I agree. I should have thought that Herbert and Crashaw had committed themselves thoroughly to the particular religious world of their choosing, even though Donne, Marvell, and Browne might bear out the remark. I should prefer to be more general and to say that in the early seventeenth century, until the Civil War forced men unnaturally to commit themselves and to take sides, they had an exceptional number of options open to them and that they throve on these options whether or not they ultimately settled to a definite habit of mind.

My final question is: how far did Milton share the prevailing intellectual freedom of his age and how far did he, in his own way, succeed in doing the kind of thing that we consider the Metaphysical poets to have been good at?

I can be brief in answering the first question. It is fairly well agreed that in his early poems Milton showed himself open to many sides of the life of the time. Though favouring the Puritan wing of the Anglican church he had a taste for stained-glass windows and choral music; though believing in the rule of moderation he wrote rapturously of the bounties of nature; though hostile to gluttony he allowed himself a gaudy day in gay company once a month; and so on. And, on the intellectual side he had, like Donne, an unquenchable thirst for knowledge, ransacking the ancients but on the watch for anything new in mathematics, studying history up to his own day, and excited by reports of contemporary travel. More remarkable, his exposure to varied worlds persists in *Paradise Lost*. He did not give them the same relative degrees of honour and affection he once did; but he somehow succeeded in carrying into the new age of the Restoration the multiplicity of concerns that marked the previous age. In some ways he added to it. But I do not wish to follow this topic since I have written on it in my book on the English epic. Instead I wish to ask whether Milton simply does not compete with the turns, surprises, and ingenuities through which the Metaphysicals expressed their vitality or whether in some less obvious way he achieves their equivalent.

No one will presume to maintain that he competes openly or that Grierson ought to have included more Milton than he did in his anthology of the Meta- physicals. But I believe that he both commanded the material for competing, and did actually compete in a covert way, to an extent that is not always recognised. I have already given examples (from the *Nativity Ode* and *Lycidas*) of Milton's argument taking temporarily a backward turn, but there is also proof absolute of Milton's only too intimate knowledge of the state of mind that turns agonisingly this way and that and fails to reach a decision. I refer to Adam's long speech in the tenth book of *Paradise Lost* after the angels, at God's bidding, have twisted the even poise of the earth and produced inclemency in the air, and Discord and Death have been let loose among the beasts. It is then that Adam perceives the full significance of his crime: his own upsetting of order duplicated in animate nature and among the beasts. He tries one avenue of escape after another in prolonged and passionate argument, only to find them closed, and ends with the words:

> O conscience, into what abyss of fears
> And horrors hast thou driv'n me; out of which
> I find no way, from deep to deeper plung'd!

Milton was not 'subtle to plague himself' and he is too much in earnest about Adam's terrors to enjoy the mere processes of thought by which the full scope of these terrors is revealed. But the thought is complicated and full, and the terrors carry conviction. It was the morbid will to keep on plaguing himself that was lacking, not the materials so to do. Milton was not the man to enjoy bathing in the Slough of Despond. He was acquainted with it, and the main thing was to get out; as Adam was destined to do very soon after he had despaired of any such thing.

Not only had Milton too thrustful a temperament to dwell on the processes of thought, but he had a strong reason for not spending too much energy in loading the lyric. Although he dallied with the idea of putting a great deal into a series of high, Pindaric, odes, there is little doubt that his epic ambitions go back to his undergraduate time. It was to them principally that he directed both his learning and his poetical technique. Now the kind of small-scale wit and surprise that can delight in the lyric soon sickens in the long poem, just as the euphuism of Lyly's *Campaspe* is more successful than the same euphuism prolonged in its title-book. I wonder how many folk read the *whole* of Donne's *Anniversaries* for pleasure; that is, read it in the only way that possesses the virtue of durability. Pieces of the *Anniversaries* are highly enjoyable; it is possible to read them through as a task, or because you are interested in the thought, or because you have acquired an interest in Donne as a person and can assimilate anything he wrote on account of that special interest. But I do not believe that Donne's *Anniversaries* any more than Blake's Prophetic Books will ever rank among those works which the intelligent amateur with no axe to grind reads from end to end with growing pleasure. And the simple reason is that Donne's habit of surprise, admirable in the *Songs and Sonnets*, admirable even in as long a piece as the Third Satire, becomes deadly when prolonged. And if you want to see what abysses of dullness the prolongation of attempted wit can fall into, take a morning off your ordinary duties and devote it to the steady perusal of Davenant's *Gondibert*. To return to Milton; if he aimed at a long poem he had little inducement to cultivate a loaded and complicated form of lyric which could only lead away from or damage those aims.

But if Milton knew he must avoid the small-scale surprises of the Metaphysical lyric, this does not mean that he disapproved of other kinds of surprise, proper to the epic. Quite the contrary. He practised two kinds of surprise in *Paradise Lost*; and if he was indebted to any source for these—and in large part he may simply have been following the lead of his own instincts and preferences—his own age provided one and Aristotle the other. I will examine the two kinds of surprise, the contemporary and the Aristotelian, in order.

I have argued that Donne was unique in his reluctance to reach a destination and that he preferred to elaborate his journey. But those who did regard their destination favoured not too smooth and unsensational a journey; they found it tame to travel always over carpet-ground. The classic example of the exciting journey is Marvell's *To his Coy Mistress*. There is no doubt of his intention to arrive. The *Now therefore* that begins the third and last paragraph is as emphatic as Lucretius's *quare's* and *quapropter's*. But, before that, he had crossed the grand lazy account of all the long-drawn-out courtship he would lavish on his mistress, IF there were world enough and time, with the simple and irresistible turn from make-believe to reality, from a faked leisure to the terrifying truth of present urgency:

> But at my back I always hear
> Time's winged chariot hurrying near:
> And yonder all before us lie
> Deserts of vast eternity.

That is the kind of surprise which the age encouraged Marvell to fabricate and which makes the age's poetry so wonderfully attractive. With perhaps a less sensational technique, but no less surely, Milton is a master of the same sort of surprise.

It is time to illustrate, and I choose a famous passage from the first book of *Paradise Lost* (730-52) describing the fall of the architect of Pandemonium. Milton gives us part of his history. He had put his architectural skill to good use in his unfallen days in heaven and later he became the god of fire and metal work of the Greeks and Romans under the names of Hephaestus, Vulcan, or (and this is the one Milton uses) Mulciber. Homer, in a comic passage in the first book in the *Iliad* (a passage occurring in a place in that book closely corresponding to the place of Milton's passage), recounts how after an angry scene in Olympus Zeus quelled with his threats the violent temper of Hera, his own wife and mother of Hephaestus. Hephaestus tells his mother to cheer up and says it is no good resisting Zeus, when he means business. And he reminds her of *his* experience. Zeus in his anger caught him by the foot and threw him out of Olympus. He travelled all day and, as the sun set, fell on the island of Lemnos. And there was little breath left in him. Milton repeats this story of Hephaestus or Mulciber (with significant changes) and then hints that Homer's story is a garbled version of the fall of one of the devils from Heaven. Here is the passage. Milton has just described the building of Pandemonium, its oriental splendour and its brilliant artificial lighting, and he goes on:

> The hasty multitude
> Admiring entered, and the work some praise

And some the architect: his hand was known
In heav'n by many a towered structure high,
Where sceptred angels held their residence
And sat as princes, whom the supreme King
Exalted to such power and gave to rule,
Each in his hierarchy, the orders bright.
Nor was his name unheard or unadored
In ancient Greece; and in Ausonian land
Men called him Mulciber; and how he fell
From heav'n they fabled, thrown by angry Jove
Sheer o'er the crystal battlements: from morn
To noon he fell, from noon to dewy eve,
A summer's day; and with the setting sun
Dropped from the zenith like a falling star
On Lemnos, th' Aegean isle. This they relate
Erring: for he with this rebellious rout
Fell long before; nor aught availed him now
To have built in heav'n high towers, nor did
      he scape
By all his engines but was headlong sent
With his industrious crew to build in hell.

I could use this passage to illustrate how easily Milton passes from the oriental to the classical, from the classical to the patristic (for it was the Fathers of the church who equated the devils of Christian mythology with the gods of the Greek); but this is not the point I most wish to make. The lines I am really concerned with now are those describing the fall of Mulciber. In the Homeric original there is nothing about the summer's day, or morn and dewy eve, or the falling star. Why should Milton have added these? He did so for the very reasons that made Marvell construct his *Coy Mistress* as he did: in order to delight through surprise, through adding another dimension. Milton has built up a vast, artificial, pretentious effect in recounting the various engineering and architectural feats of the devils; and now he suddenly introduces scenes of real life, morning and noon of a perfect summer's day, and the beauty of a shooting star in the cool of evening. It is like the sudden opening of a casement followed by the sudden crash of closing it with the word *erring*. But for a few moments healthy sunlight and cool dew break in on the colossally imagined artificial light and cruel heat of Milton's hell. And this suddenness is the Miltonic counterpart of the feats of verbal wit practised by the Metaphysicals. The modern parallel that occurs to me is the breaking in of the Renaissance, Giorgione-like picture into the asceticism of Eliot's *Ash-Wednesday*.

At the first turning of the third stair
Was a slotted window bellied like a fig's fruit
And beyond the hawthorn blossom and a pasture scene
The broadbacked figure drest in blue and green
Enchanted the maytime with an antique flute.

For another example turn to the end of *Paradise Lost*. Into the terrifying picture of the angels thrusting Adam and Eve out of their garden-home Milton inserted the utterly quotidian picture of a farm labourer walking home to supper:

So spake our mother, Eve, and Adam heard
Well pleased, but answered not; for now too nigh

Th' archangel stood, and from the other hill
To their fixt station, all in bright array,
The Cherubim descended, on the ground
Gliding meteorous, as evening mist
Ris'n from a river o'er the marish glides
And gathers ground fast at the labourer's heel
Homeward returning.

Of course we know why Milton made this insertion:
he wanted to bring his cosmic action to rest in simple
humanity. But the magnitude of the surprise and the
wonder of this manifestation of wit are not lessened
on account of their perfect congruity with Milton's
design. And such examples of large-scale wit are proper
to the age in which Milton lived. The age helped him
to achieve them in a way the Romantic age, for instance,
could never have done.

I come finally to the second kind of surprise that
Milton exploited; and it is of a much more comprehensive kind, the Aristotelian process of complicating
a plot by means of *anagnorisis* and *peripeteia*, which
L. J. Potts in his brave and original translation of the
Poetics renders as *disclosure* and *irony*. Aristotle made it
clear that the same principles governed both epic and
tragedy; and if, as he does, Milton mentioned Aristotle
in his preface to *Samson Agonistes*, we can be sure that
he had him in mind when he wrote his two long
narratives. Even in *Paradise Regained*, itself so unclassical
and uncomplicated, he introduces the Aristotelian irony
of events near the end. Satan, having placed Christ on a
pinnacle of the Temple, tells him to throw himself down:

To whom thus Jesus, 'Also it is written,
Tempt not the Lord thy God'. He said, and stood.
But Satan, smitten with amazement, fell.

That is the Aristotelian irony or reversal. Satan intended Christ to fall; but instead he fell himself; and in so doing he recognised him as his superior, the son of God. In *Samson Agonistes* Samson thinks he is lost when all the time he is saved; the reverse of the situation in *Oedipus the King* where Oedipus thinks someone else the cause of the plague in the city and discovers it is himself.

But the greatest of Milton's ironies is in *Paradise Lost*. Milton in referring to it openly hardly does its complexity full justice. The reference comes early in the poem when Satan is about to rise from the lake of fire. Milton tells us that God allowed Satan to rise so that in the end he

enraged might see
How all his malice serv'd but to bring forth
Infinite goodness, grace and mercy shown
On man by him seduced but on himself
Treble confusion, wrath, and vengeance poured.

Satan thought that when Adam and Eve had sinned they were bound to be lost for good as he was when he sinned. He had failed to estimate the relative sins of himself and of the human pair justly and found that what he had plotted for evil turned out good. This is the chief irony of the poem; and it is matched by the construction. The losing of Paradise through the eating of the apple seems to be the climax; but the true climax is when Adam and Eve admit good feelings into their hearts and by repentance gain the hope of another paradise. And there are other, subsidiary, ironies or reversals. Eve and to a lesser extent Adam were persuaded through the serpent's agency to think that by eating the apple they would mount in the order of creation, instead of which they sank lower within their own order. They also *recognised* that the serpent was not wise but the tempter. All this is within the larger irony. And there is the third irony that Adam and Eve confess themselves lost and sinning and fail to realise that through this very confession they are actually on the way to being saved. These grand structural workings are too vast to allow the word 'wit' to be applied to them but they are analogous to the smaller scale surprises to which that word can be properly applied. And even if they have their warrant in the *Poetics* of Aristotle they are perfectly in harmony with the richness of thought and feeling that makes the seventeenth century uniquely attractive to the temper of our own complicated and incongruous age.

.   .   .   .   .

I began these lectures by hinting that I might present a pattern of oppositions and congruences in the poetry (mainly lyrical) of the earlier seventeenth century rather different from the usual one. But I have done no more than make some scattered observations, for to outline a pattern, even if I could do it (which is doubtful), would take far too long. My hope is that these observations may lead to others, as: that Cowley, though he

F   73

came under the spell of Donne's rhetoric, was not at all like him but in essential character was more like Waller; or that Herrick, though not under the spell of Donne's rhetoric, was more like Carew, who was so, than like Waller, who was not.

On the two main figures, Milton and Donne, I have been more definite and I can state the gist of my opinion as follows. Milton was a great figure looking back to the Middle Ages and forward to the spirit and the achievements of eighteenth-century puritanism. But his larger surprises and ironies are in harmony with the requirements of his age and of course are largely inspired by them. He was very much of a person, yet he did not thrust his personality overmuch into his poetry and he chose to inhabit the general centre rather than to construct a private bower, or perform dazzling acrobatics, near the circumference. He is more like Jonson and Marvell than he is like Donne and Crashaw. Donne, on the other hand, was a great innovator but with a narrower, more personal talent. He made people heed him, he stirred them up, he contributed to the age's vitality. But he remains the exception, and his admirers will do him no good in the long run if they pretend he was anything else.

APPENDICES

DONNE'S SONNET
SINCE SHE WHOM I LOV'D

I wrote in my text as if I were certain of the meaning of every word of this sonnet. But this is not so, for two passages continue to perplex me. Line 10 used to be obscure in the editions when punctuated *Dost woo my soul for hers; offring all thine:* with the semi-colon removed and a comma after *soul,* as printed in the texts of Roger E. Bennett and Helen Gardner, it is plain and effective. The remaining difficulties occur in lines 2 and 9. I take them in turn.

Line 2. Does *and to hers* go with *To Nature* before, or with *and my good is dead* after? Helen Gardner assumes the second, admits a difficulty of sense, and offers alternative explanations. Until I read her note I assumed without question that *to hers* was parallel to *To Nature* and that the line meant that Donne's wife had given back her body to Nature and had rendered her last service to her kin, and that Donne's prosperity has in consequence departed. This explanation has at least the advantage of grammar, for *her* not *hers* would, strictly, be required for the other sense. That, however, is a very minor point; and readers will be wise to allow the run of the verse to settle their preference. It is mainly because I think the prosody of the lines as I explain them superior that I think as I do.

Line 9. Of whom does Donne beg more love? Helen Gardner, whom I have consulted, is quite sure that it is of God. If God has fed his thirst and Donne is dropsical he will go on craving more of God's love for ever. This may be right, and it is indeed the more obvious explanation.

Nevertheless, in reading uninfluenced by others' opinions I took the *holy thirsty dropsy* of line 8 to be for the wife. It is now a holy love, because the wife is in heaven. If at this place in the sonnet Donne has abandoned definitively the desire of his wife's love, there is no point in God's jealousy later in the sonnet and in the reference to saints and angels in line 12. His wife is one of these saints. Donne knows that his craving for the love of his dead wife is rightly destined to be supplanted and overwhelmed by the boundless love of God, but there is a poetic gain in his confessing to the difficulty and delay of this destiny.

DONNE'S *EXTASIE*

No one would gainsay the usual description of Donne's *Extasie* as one of his greatest metaphysical love-poems. Yet I doubt if that description points us to the things the poem most concerns. It does nothing to explain Donne's insistence on self-knowledge; and his interest in the 'that subtile knot, which makes us man'. Further (and this is heretical) the actual love-trance is pretty coolly described; it is rather an academic affair. Donne's emotions are more deeply engaged elsewhere. His real interest is in the basic constitution of man and man's place in the order of creation.

To an age versed in religious technique there was nothing strange in the mystical state of *ecstasis*. It is a single item in Browne's resounding list at the end of *Urn Burial* of

> Christian Annihilation, *Ecstasis*, Exsolution, Liquefaction, Transformation, the kiss of the Spouse, Gustation of God, and Ingression into the Divine shadow.

Marvell in the *Garden* assumes that the reader is perfectly familiar with the idea when he makes his soul leave his body and perch on a tree like a bird. And here is a prose description of the state written in the early seventeenth century, and like Donne's poem faithfully recording its traditional characteristics: [1]

> Though the present condition of man bee earthly, made of the earth, feeds on the earth, and is dissolved to the earth, and therefore the soule doth lesse discover her selfe by her proper actions, then doth the materiall body; yet it is not unknowne to

[1] From Christopher Goodman, *The Fall of Man* (1616), 42.

79

Philosophie, that there is an extasis of the soule, wherein she is carried in a trance, wholly and only intending the intellectuall functions, while the body lies dead like a carcasse without breath, sense, motion, or nourishment, onely as a pledge to assure us of the soules returne.

Reading the *Extasie* we are in fact in a world not of violent innovation, but of tradition; and the total poem exploits something much more central to traditional lore than the specialised state of a mystical experience.

When the ages of Spenser and Donne considered man they associated him with his cosmic setting in a way strange to a modern. He was still part of the great order which the Middle Ages had succeeded in imposing on the universe. That order was pictured in three main forms: a chain of being, a set of corresponding and multifariously connected planes, and a dance. In the chain of being man occupied a key-position between the beasts and the angels, uniting in himself three souls, vegetative, sensitive, and rational, and by the freedom of his will having the power to incline in one or other direction. As one of the planes of creation he was a little world corresponding in much detail with the heavenly orders, the universe or macrocosm, and the state or body politic. In the order of his social and political setting he took part in the great dance of the cosmos.

As the microcosm man shared mere existence with minerals, the power of growth with vegetables, and the power of feeling with animals. His peculiar attribute was the reason, peculiar in the way he could use it, but shared by the angels and the quality through which he was the image of God. Human reason was divided into the two great faculties of the understanding or 'wit' and the will. Man fulfilled his proper function as man by exercising these faculties properly. In this exercise he was separated from beasts and angels alike. Bestial understanding was limited though it did exist, as Donne himself said in the *Nocturnall upon S. Lucies Day.*

> I should preferre,
> If I were any beast,
> Some ends, some means.

Angelic understanding was perfected, for every angel possessed all the knowledge his faculties were capable of holding. As for the will, the beasts were entirely ruled by the stars, while the angelic will, though free, was simply equated with the will of God. Only in man were understanding and will variable.

With such possibilities of change in understanding and will it followed that education or 'nurture' was of the highest moment. It was the special function of man to learn. What should he learn to know? God, of course. But best indirectly. God can be easiest understood *per speculum creaturarum.* But even that great means had not quite the standing of the other, the knowledge of self. Of all human functions self-knowledge was the most typical and the most important: impossible for the beasts, unnecessary for the angels, but for man the supreme moral function. When Regan says to Goneril that their father has known himself but slenderly she is calling him a child, uneducated, one who has hardly begun to do the proper job of a man.

Some of the above utter commonplaces form the main theme of Donne's *Extasie.* The argument is that through the different acts of love the function of man as man is being worthily performed.

81

First there is the position of man between beast and angel. The lovers aspire to the purely intellectual and disembodied state of the angels, and their souls leave their bodies in a dumb and motionless trance. (There is nothing romantic about the lovers' dumbness in this poem.) But at the end of the poem they recognise their human limitations and the need of the body and of the senses (which they share with the beasts). If the blood, the main vital agent of the body, strives upwards through the three kinds of spirits it engenders (natural vital and animal) to the meeting place of body and soul, 'that subtile knot, which makes us man', so must the intellectual principle, the soul, be ready to co-operate and on its side to climb down the ladder of being to the region of the senses. Otherwise, great Prince though the soul be, it will yet lack scope and be a prisoner.

Nevertheless the ecstasy though temporary has done its work: it has 'unperplexed' or untied 'that subtile knot' and in so doing has made the strands clearer to the view. More precisely it has been an exercise in education; it has advanced the great human function of self-knowledge.

This Extasie doth unperplex
(We said) and tell us what we love,
Wee see by this, it was not sexe,
We see, we saw not what did move.

Through the ecstasy the lovers now realise that they had lacked self-knowledge before: now they know that sex was not the motive. Later on the lovers' souls claim to have reached a degree of self-knowledge beyond any possible reach in an ordinary single soul. In the ordinary state a soul is 'perplext', so tied up with the fickle body that utter self-knowledge is out of the question; but this union of two ecstatic souls into an oversoul *does* know itself. It is composed of changeless things, which can be steadily apprehended and studied.

> Wee then, who are this new soule, know,
> Of what we are compos'd, and made,
> For, th'Atomies of which we grow,
> Are soules, whom no change can invade.

This is the main theme: man's place and function in creation's scale. But though the cosmic dance is omitted (unless one likes to include the cosmic music in the reference to spheres and Intelligences), the corresponding planes are hinted at. The 'pregnant bank' at the opening refers forward to physical love at the end and suggests the duplication of erotic function in microcosm and nature. The string that unites the lovers' eyes is double in that it runs from one pair to another pair of eyes, but it is 'one'. And it would be (roughly) circular. As such it would correspond to the natural motion of heavenly things, which was not as with the elements up and down but an eternal round: the motion of the soul itself.[1] The angels or Intelligences guiding the heavenly spheres correspond to the soul guiding the body; macrocosm and microcosm again. As the prince is in the state so is the soul in the body and the mental functions of man: body politic and microcosm.

To maintain that the *Extasie* deals with the nature of man rather than with a specialised and extraordinary love experience is not to cry down the poem. It is rather to enlarge its content and to relate it to a great tragic theme, to Shakespeare when he makes Hamlet compare man to beast and angel, and Lear retort to his daughters—

[1] This interpretation of the string is of course conjectural; I don't want to press it.

83

Allow not nature more than nature needs,
Man's life is cheap as beast's.

Of course the *Extasie* is in some sort a love-poem, but I cannot take it either as the expression of hectic passion or as a cynical attempt at seduction. It shows us Donne at his sanest and comparatively detached from his object. It has the cool strong rhythms of *A Valediction Forbidding Mourning* rather than the stormy rhythms of the other *Valediction of Weeping*. And as for sanity, it allows a healthy scope for the body in subordination to the mind which is quite opposed to Donne's terrible outbursts in the *Second Anniversary*:

Thinke that no stubborne sullen Anchorit,
Which fixt to a pillar, or a grave, doth sit
Bedded, and bath'd in all his ordures, dwels
So fowly as our Soules in their first-built Cels.

The *Extasie* shows us love as a part of the great human business of living as human beings should.

INDEX

INDEX

87